No Excuses

No Excuses
Antonio Sabáto Jr.
Workout for Life

PRINCIPAL PHOTOGRAPHY BY GREG GORMAN

ADDITIONAL PHOTOGRAPHY BY BRIAN TO

WITH TEXT CONTRIBUTIONS BY GREG FREITAS

UNIVERSE

Published in the United States of America in 1999 by Universe Publishing

A Division of Rizzoli International Publications, Inc., 300 Park Avenue South

New York, NY 10010

99 00 01 02 / 10 9 8 7 6 5 4 3 2 1

Printed in Italy

Library of Congress Catalog Card Number: 99–71282

This book is dedicated to Joe Sanceri, to God, to my son, Jack, and to my father, Antonio Senior. Most important, to Batman and to my friend Robert (Bobby) DiAngelo.

I'd like to thank all of the people who made this book possible: **Joe Sanceri,** my trainer, for all of his help. My gym, **Private Exercise,** 11911 Washington Boulevard, Los Angeles, CA 90066, (310) 915-1191. **Chris Steele**, and everyone at Steele Boxer, 2907 Washington Boulevard, Marina Del Rey, CA 90292, (310) 827-2697. **Greg Freitas, Greg Gorman,** and **Brian To** for their contributions. **Keya Khayatian, Tracy Steinsapir,** and **Susan Culley** for helping set this up. **Nike, Fila, Adidas,** and **Parke** & **Ronen** for dressing me so well. Finally, thanks to **Charles Miers, Margaret Braver,** and everyone else at **Universe** who guided me through this whole process.

contents

A New Approach to Fitness

Our country has been obsessed with fitness for quite a while. It seems like there's a new gym on every corner, and anyone can join—gym training isn't just for professional athletes and fitness fanatics, it's for everybody.

Scientists refine the fields of diet and exercise constantly, introducing new equipment and supplements all the time. Our knowledge and our concern with proper nutrition increases every year, and as a result the supermarkets are stocked with fat-free foods.

So why are Americans in worse shape year after year?

The answers are simple and obvious. Most Americans don't eat right and they don't exercise. If they do watch what they eat, it's only sporadically: a strict diet may be followed by weeks of splurging, causing the need for yet another quick-fix diet. A program to look good for summer can be completely destroyed during the holiday season. And if they do exercise, they're following the pack, picking up bad habits along the way.

Even more alarming, some people have decided that fitness isn't for them. They see it as an activity solely for professional athletes or vain bodybuilders. They embrace the notion that they are couch potatoes, thinking that it's okay to be overweight and sluggish because our society has grown to accept that.

What isn't so obvious is what can be done to change all that. We know what needs to be done and yet we find every reason why we can't do it. We're filled with excuses.

Everyone has excuses for not getting in shape, and by now we've heard them all. We don't have enough time, we can't get motivated, or it just isn't necessary to eat well and exercise. The list goes on and on. **This book won't help you to conquer those excuses until you decide you're ready to listen and learn.** If you still want to follow the easiest route to maintaining a healthy body, you'll dismiss this book. **But if you're ready to make an improvement, this book will provide a blueprint for achieving lasting fitness. It will help you to not only look good, but to be healthy for the rest of your life.**

Over the past three years I have developed a system for maintaining my own body with my friend and trainer Joe Sanceri. Joe has been involved with fitness and weight training since the 1940s. He's seen and tried just about every program that's come along in the last fifty years. He knows what works and what doesn't, because he's tried it himself and on others. The program that we've developed is based on his vast experience and knowledge, and it can work as well for you as it has for me.

Joe has become disillusioned over the years with the techniques and practices that have come from the bodybuilding community. They advocate an overly muscular body that's not even attractive to one percent of the population. The other ninety-nine percent want to look lean, firm, and toned. **We want long, flexible muscles, not huge, bulging muscles.** Pick up any fitness magazine and you'll see the excessively muscle-bound look I'm talking about. Chances are the man or woman on the cover displays an enormous musculature. Chances are they probably have trouble buying clothes off the rack, too. **Most people exercise because they want to fit into a suit or a dress; most bodybuilders wear drawstring pants because they can't fit into anything else.**

I have a lot of respect for bodybuilders and the intensity they bring to their training. There is much that we can learn from them. It's an extremely exhausting and competitive sport and the ones who are truly successful have unbelievable stamina and willpower. It's just not attractive to the rest of the population—and it's certainly not healthy. Our program is designed for the other ninety-nine percent. It's a program for true mass appeal.

A complete workout: Do both at the same time.

One myth that people have adopted is that weight training and cardio vascular fitness need to be separate activities. The typical workout might start with a few minutes of stretching, followed by weightlifting, then thirty minutes or more of cardio. Two hours later you're finally finished and wondering when you'll ever have time to work out again.

The foundation of our program is the superset, combining two or more exercises into a larger set, and then combining even more different exercises with those. This allows us to make cardiovascular gains as well because we're lifting virtually nonstop.

Since traditional weightlifting is based on lifting as much weight as you can, resting is constantly required between sets. We all have plenty of time away from the gym to rest. There are very few of us with such strenuous lives that our muscles don't rest when we are away from the

gym. So the time spent inside the gym should be spent on nonstop training. By combining all of our lifts into supersets we maximize what we can accomplish with our time.

The key is moderate weight. If you lift so much weight that you don't use correct form, you won't properly contract your muscles and you'll need more time to recover. You'll fall into the trap of resting between sets. Your heart rate will fall while you're resting and you won't get the cardiovascular workout that comes from a continuous, flowing workout.

When we combine weight training and cardiovascular exercise into one continuous program, we not only make more improvement, we do it in less time. The next time you go to the gym, look around and pick out someone who is starting at about the same time. While they're plodding along, resting between sets, you'll be working nonstop, improving the entire time. By the time you're finished, they'll still be there and they won't have accomplished half as much as you have.

Getting fitness back on track.

Back in the 1950s and 1960s, when Joe and his buddies trained at Muscle Beach, the fitness world was a small, close-knit group. Those guys lived the fitness lifestyle around the clock. Training advances were made through trial and error. Discoveries were passed around by word-of-mouth and put to use on the sand and on the stage. This is not to paint a rosy picture but to point out that they did what they did because they appreciated training for its own sake. They had the desire to improve the body every day.

In the 1970s, the fitness movement spread from the cult fringe to the mainstream. By the time the 1980s rolled around, fitness had become a class system. Belonging to an **expensive gym** was like joining a country club, athletic gear became a **status symbol,** and fitness became a billion-dollar industry.

The 1990s have seen an explosion of scientific research in the world of fitness. **Chemicals** with unpronounceable names have flooded the shelves of every nutrition store, their labels promising to give people that "extra edge." We all need an edge. But what the nutrition experts don't tell us is that the extra edge doesn't come in a bottle, it comes from within. Developing an intensity, a hunger for improvement in everything you do, is worth more than anything that comes from a lab.

Looking for an edge through chemicals is just another excuse. If you think you won't make the same advances unless you have this machine or try that diet—that's an excuse. ***The only thing you need to achieve fitness is your body, what you put into it, and the effort you make. We don't need to use science as a crutch, because we have everything we need within ourselves.***

Another of the destructive attitudes that permeate the fitness world is fad mentality. People are always looking for the next big thing. Whether it's some new extreme diet, or an obscure fitness machine advertised on late-night television, these fads capture the public's imagination, fooling us into thinking we can get something for nothing. But when those fads don't work, the public has only itself to blame.

It's true that many of these fads can still have some beneficial effects on our fitness— that's part of their allure. And doing something is always preferable to the alternative. The problem is that **the fad mentality has replaced the work mentality.**

The need to sell products, to sell magazines, to sell equipment has given us a multitude of self-proclaimed experts whose next paycheck depends on promoting what they have to sell. These people aren't selling you their products because they're good for you, they're selling them to make a profit. People have made millions of dollars and built business empires by capitalizing on the fitness boom. Yet at the same time, overall fitness has declined. Just because someone is a good businessman doesn't mean that he's looking out for your health.

Everything you need to know about staying in shape for the rest of your life is contained in this book. That's because getting in shape isn't complicated. It doesn't come in a bottle or an expensive package. It's common sense, and most important, it's commitment.

There is only one way.

Fitness fads keep us from realizing one truth: there is only one way to stay fit, and that will never change.

Exercise regularly and eat healthful foods in moderation. It doesn't get much simpler than that. Then do it every day for the rest of your life. Doesn't seem so easy anymore, does it? Everyone knows how to do it. You don't need books and magazines to tell you that. But it isn't easy; in fact, it's very hard. That's part of what makes it so worthwhile. That's why so few people are in good shape. Most people would rather do it the easy way, which is like not doing it at all.

What is the new approach to fitness? Getting back to basics. Using common sense. Listening when your body tells you what it needs, not what you read in a magazine or hear from some guy at the gym. It's time to stop making excuses and start taking responsibility for our own health and fitness.

Making a Lifelong Commitment

The key to health and fitness is consistency. There have been plenty of people over the years that have seen what Joe and I accomplish in the gym. They're eager to try it. So they come into the gym full of enthusiasm that first day. By the end of the first session though, most of them are ready to go back to their old ways. The ones who do stick around are finished after the first week or shortly thereafter.

My exercise program isn't any more difficult than a lot of other programs. What is difficult is having the desire to stick with it. This is the biggest training obstacle that we can overcome.

Most people lack the commitment to get into shape. We live in a fast-food world, and most people take a fast-food approach to fitness. We want quick answers and even faster results. And if it doesn't happen fast enough, we look for other ways to do it. We're all too ready to try the next quick fix in a long series of easy answers.

Take a peek at the local magazine rack. "Six weeks to a thinner you." "Get in shape for summer." The problem with these headlines is that fitness should not be a short-term goal. ***Forget about six weeks from now; we're thinking ten, twenty, thirty years ahead. The only time frame that matters in fitness is how long we live. We want to live as long as possible and be fit the entire time. Start making choices that will pay off for the rest of your life.***

"I'll do it later." "I'll worry about it when I get older." More excuses. The only way to build

for the future is to take care of it right now. There are few things that are guaranteed in life. But I guarantee that if you get in shape now and make the commitment to stay that way, you won't regret it for a second.

Your body knows what it needs to do.

We know when we need to get into shape. Our body tells us, giving us constant feedback, sending countless messages every day. It tells us when it's hungry, when it's in pain, when we need to back off, and when we can push it to the limit. **If your aerobic conditioning is off, your body responds with shortness of breath. If you're overweight, you're constantly reminded by the way your clothes fit (or don't) and the way you move. If you need more strength, your body tells you, whether through a regular difficulty in performing everyday tasks or through constant nagging injuries, such as lower back pain.**

It's easier to destroy than to build.

Every action has a consequence. **But to our bodies the actions and their consequences aren't always equal. What takes months to build can be destroyed in a week.** This is why on-off conditioning never works. The time off erases everything we accomplish during the time on.

That's why we must vow to come back every day, and to recognize that we need to compensate for any time off. If the demands of my schedule force me to cut back on my training, that means I need to eat that much better. Because once we've lost it, getting it back is that much tougher. **Stay on top of your conditioning; it isn't something you can easily catch up on later.**

A workout for life.

Joe and I wanted to develop a program that would be effective for men and women of any age. I used to do some competitive kickboxing, training with Chris Steele in Marina Del Rey for years. But as much as I still love the martial arts, I couldn't continue to do that as my primary workout. I wanted to find an exercise program that would work my heart and lungs, burn calories, and make me stronger. And I wanted it to be a program that I could follow for the rest of my life.

The exercise plan we've devised is an ideal workout for women. Most women are interested in fat-burning exercises that increase muscle tone without adding size. By maintaining a proper diet, women can lift weights without fear of bulking up.

And by working out with low resistance, women can get all the benefits of aerobic exercise and weight training at the same time.

Whether you choose to use the program that Joe and I have developed or if you prefer some other safe, well-established method, it really doesn't matter. Just choose something that works, and do it for the rest of your life.

Why I Do What I Do

I care about my health and the way I look and feel. I realize that I only get one body and I'm determined to take care of it. So I train hard. I'm proud of it and I don't apologize for it.

Don't let people slow you down by trying to make you feel guilty for taking care of yourself. There is a small group of people that will call you vain, selfish, or worse because you care about your body. These people seem to think that sitting around and doing nothing is the way to live your life. Surely it's an easy way, but we do nothing to honor and respect our bodies when all we do is the minimum required to survive.

Just breathing isn't good enough.

A wonderful gift has been given to each of us: the human body is the ultimate machine, more valuable than the fastest race car or the sleekest jet. We need to care for it as such.

You wouldn't put junk in the tank of your car because that would ruin it. Yet humans put the most terrible things into their bodies. We take better care of our cars than we do of ourselves. Just breathing isn't good enough; we need to do more.

Another excuse: since no one knows how long they'll live, fitness training is a waste of time. The opposite is true. We could all die tomorrow, so we must take care of today. Our health is precious, and we shouldn't leave it to chance. We should do everything within our power to give ourselves the best odds for a long and productive life. We owe it to ourselves and to our families. It's our responsibility as members of society and as human beings.

Success is not a gift.

Another excuse that people use is genetics. I'm too big, I'll never get bigger, I'm short, or I'm tall—whatever it might be. Genetics does determine many things, but does that mean we're sup-

posed to stop trying? Genetics doesn't determine desire, it doesn't determine whether or not we get the most out of what God has given us. Maximize your own potential. Don't worry about what life has given you, worry about what you have given back. Be the best version of yourself that you can be.

Successful people weren't born that way: some were born with advantages and others with disadvantages, just like everybody else. **Success comes from relentless hard work. It's not a gift, and it isn't ours to keep. We will only stay successful as long as we're willing to work for it.**

Train like an athlete.

A pro football player knows that if he doesn't train in the off-season he's liable to get injured. An NBA player has to be in shape all the time or he might be out of a job. We're no different from them. They may run faster and jump higher, but when it comes to standards of health and longevity, we're all the same. We all have just one body, and we can use it or lose it. Just because they get paid for it doesn't give them more reason to take care of themselves.

My friends who are former football players tell me that the way I train is as intense as anything they've seen. I don't do it because I have to go to the stadium every Sunday to play. I've got a far more important game than that, just as we all do. We all have to wake up every morning and be the best person we can be.

Whether you're an actor or a teacher or a truck driver, you can train like an athlete. Why deny yourself the benefits of the intense training that athletes engage in just because you're not getting paid for it? Though it's nothing but an excuse, we hear it constantly: "If they paid me that kind of money I'd be in the gym all the time." Then why are there so many overweight "athletes" in every professional sport? There are countless pros getting paid millions to stay in shape who simply can't do it. The promise of a big paycheck is an empty incentive—our own personal reasons for getting in shape are much more effective motivations.

We can show up to work out every day just like a pro athlete would, even if we're not getting paid. We can bring the same intensity and state of mind as a guy getting ready for the big game—we just have to want it as much.

"Out of shape" is no longer an excuse.

Our health is the one thing we have in common with every other human being. We all want to be productive and fit for the rest of our lives, and if we put in the time now we can enjoy the benefits, now and later. **By maintaining a constant level of fitness, we're ready for any opportunity that comes our way. We're never out of shape so we don't have to get back into shape.**

Being out of shape is a tough way to go through life. You climb an extra flight of stairs at work and notice your own heavy breathing. Or you take a ski vacation and wonder how you'll make it back to the mountain after lunch. Or your friends schedule a weekend basketball game and you wonder to yourself if you'll be able to keep up. You'll tell yourself the same thing: "I'm out of shape." You'll commiserate with your friends and they'll also admit, with a chuckle, that they're "out of shape."

"Out of shape" is such a common excuse it's a cliché. Remove your-self from the long list of people who use it. Start making improvement today and join those people who are ready to climb those stairs, ski that slope, take it to the hoop. Be the one who still has energy when everyone else is resorting to excuses.

      Don't train for a certain sport or a certain season. Train to be ready for anything all the time. I have a very active lifestyle and I like to be ready for any opportunity that comes my way. If I have a chance to go skiing or scuba diving I want to be prepared. **_Train like an athlete and you won't have any excuses._**

My Trainer, Joe Sanceri

I've known Joe since I was a teenager, when I used to work at the old Marina Athletic Club in Marina Del Rey, California. He was the manager and head personal trainer, and I was just a young kid working the front desk. He sensed my ambition to train intensely, and I could tell that he was the most demanding trainer in the gym. We've trained together ever since. He has devoted his entire life to fitness, and **his chief motivation has always been to help people improve their lives by getting in shape.**

A forefather of fitness.

I've always looked up to Joe, and I trust him implicitly when it comes to fitness know-how. The approach he brings to fitness is both inspiring and unique. He's been training people for fifty years, so he knows what works. **All of the advice in this book is based on the techniques Joe has developed in the years since his days on Muscle Beach.**

During the 1950s, Joe managed gyms all over Southern California for Vic Tanny. Tanny and Jack LaLanne were the fitness gurus of their day. They preached bodybuilding like a gospel and eventually opened gyms all over the country. Fitness machines as we know them hadn't been invented yet, so they did it the old-school way: by using their bodies as resistance and pumping iron. With all of the high-tech equipment and beautifully designed gyms we have today, it's easy to take for granted the dedication that these guys showed. They were considered on the "fringe" at the time, and had no idea that their way of life would become so universal.

Joe trained outdoors at the original Muscle Beach, back when it was in Santa Monica, in the 1950s. The Muscle Beach denizens trained all day long, working in gyms or taking bit parts in movies to get by. Tourists would line up on the boardwalk to take pictures and witness the unique California lifestyle of the time—and the bodybuilders gave them quite a show.

They would work out whole routines combining strength and gymnastic moves, forming human pyramids, tossing each other high in the air over people's heads. Every day it was like the circus had come to town. It was a wild time for some young men and women who were making up the **fitness revolution** as they went along. They weren't in it for money or fame. They chose fitness because they loved it. It was an exciting lifestyle filled with interesting characters.

Joe trained with the legends. He worked out with Steve Reeves, whom Joe still calls the best bodybuilder he's ever seen. (Reeves went on to play Hercules in several movies.) He worked with Joe Gold, whose name is now associated with some of the most intense, high-profile gyms in the country. He saw California beach culture turn into a worldwide phenomenon.

In the 1960s, an unsavory crowd and some criminal activity led to the downfall of

Mr. Mu
19

Joe Sanceri, second at left

Muscle Beach, so the mayor of Santa Monica wanted it out of the city. So they took their act a few miles south, down the sand to Venice Beach. This is the famous Muscle Beach we know today.

Joe first noticed steroid use around this time. He witnessed the evolution of steroid abuse, from people swallowing tiny blue pills to injecting themselves with huge needles. Over the course of thirty years, Joe took steroids as well. He's extremely grateful that he suffered no major damage as a result and he considers himself a lucky man. He lost friends to steroids, saw people ruin their lives, and saw people die.

He hasn't touched them for ten years now, and today he is an **outspoken critic of steroid use.** Joe calls for full disclosure from bodybuilding champions who exhibit their form as a model to youth, without explaining the dangerous route that made them look that way. Joe is now a devout Christian with a vast knowledge of the Bible, and we attend Grace Community Church in the Valley together.

A plan for the future.

Joe and I have trained together for a long time, but it was in February 1996 that we decided to develop **a fitness program with one goal in mind: building lifelong health and fitness.**

We knew all the components of the ideal workout. Joe had always regretted getting so big during his own training, so he wanted me **to stay lean.** Gaining size stretches your skin and causes undue strain on joints and tendons.

We'd build lean, flexible muscles, improve cardiovascular fitness, and burn calories. We also knew that **we didn't want it to consume hours of our time when five to seven hours a week would be adequate.**

This is how we decided to **make supersets the foundation of our training.** Many good trainers combine periodic supersets with conventional weight training as a way to break up the boredom of weightlifting, and make short-term gains. We realized that using supersets instead of conventional weight training would give us all of the benefits with-

04

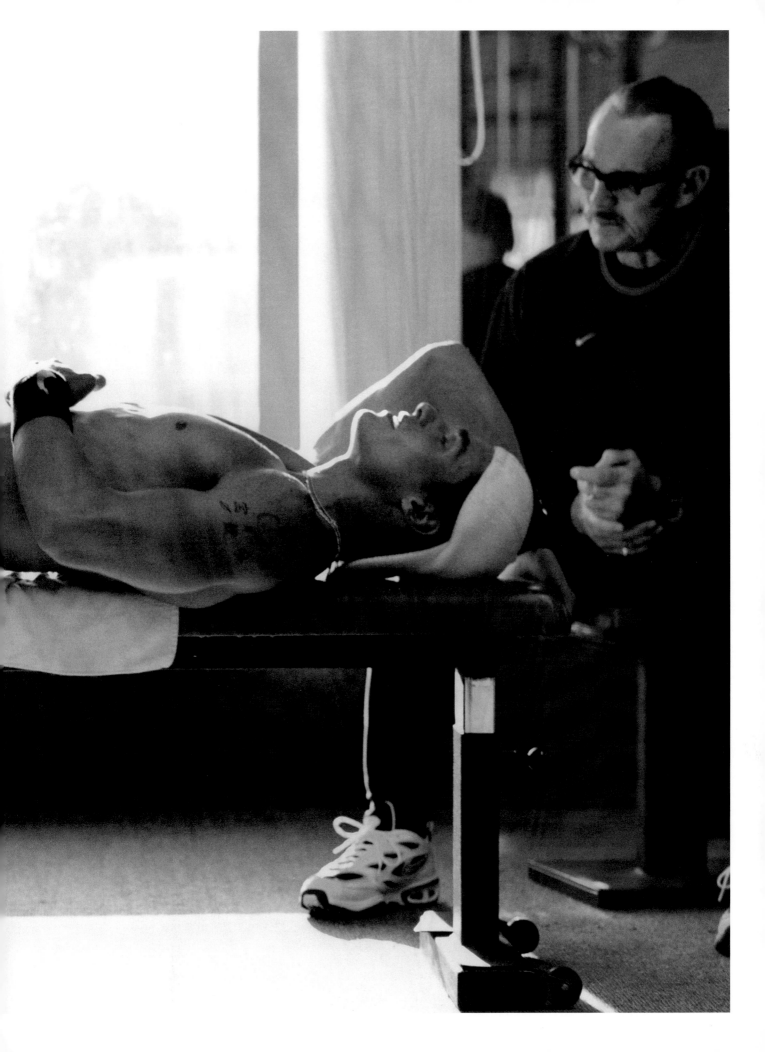

This is a picture I drew of Joe when I was seventeen.

out sacrificing a thing. We've removed much of the potential for injury, as well as the monotony that is inherent in traditional weight-training programs, and **we've added an intense, calorie-burning aerobic workout.** We don't waste a single moment when we're in the gym. It's just me and Joe, working together toward a common goal.

Make your personal trainer an equal partner.

Now Joe and I are equal partners in my training regimen. He watches every set I do, rep by rep. He keeps track of exactly what needs to be done, so that I can focus on the exercise itself. He is constantly sharing his knowledge with me during the workout, prodding me, helping me with my technique, and suggesting ways to improve.

Anyone who trains seriously should consider himself lucky to find a trainer who is as knowledgeable and as motivating as Joe. There are plenty of physical trainers out there, and some are better than others. Choosing the right one is ultimately your responsibility.

Good personal trainers can bring a lot to the workout. They should understand how each muscle functions in relation to the others, and how to build a complete, symmetrical body. They should be able to point out not only the proper technique on each exercise, but to introduce different techniques, and explain how they help us grow.

They should know every exercise in the gym—and then some. **They should be creative;** if a gym doesn't carry a particular piece of equipment that I'm used to, Joe will devise an exercise that's just as good or better. Our workout is based on doing something different every day, so Joe's vast knowledge and years of experience are crucial to the program.

Most important, personal trainers should make sure the exercise program and the training fit the person who is paying for them: you. My program will work for anyone, but it is not a routine that gets easier. We want it to get harder, so it's important to allow for constant change. Every time you see your trainer he or she should be intent on finding ways to mix it up, make it harder, and help you get better.

Interview prospective trainers.

Tell the manager of your gym that you're interested in finding a trainer that suits you, then talk to trainers until you find one you're comfortable with. Ask them about their experience. Tell them that **you want to build a workout based on increasing muscle and cardiovascular fitness at the same time,** and don't let them discourage you from implementing the training schedule that you want to carry out. Find a trainer who won't simply follow the pack. Make it clear ahead of time that you want to be pushed—and **a good trainer will push you.**

If you can't afford to have a personal trainer every day, work with one once a week, or even once a month. Bring someone into your fitness regime that has knowledge of the field and is as interested in your improvement as you are.

Even allowing a training partner to play the role of personal trainer can be helpful, especially if both of you are serious, motivated, and knowledgeable. **In the workout system Joe and I present here, you superset nonstop; therefore, two people can occupy the various machines and weights required for the supersets,** switching off when necessary.

Your Body Is Good Enough

Fitness is not technology.

The obsession with fitness has led us to steroids and supplements, fads and shortcuts. There is no reason to resort to these so-called advances in technology, because **the body itself is good enough.**

Our ideas about fitness have always been influenced by the times in which we live. So it's understandable that the information and technology age has affected how we perceive fitness. But objective standards of fitness haven't changed. We may have better ways of measuring it, but **being in shape still means being in shape.** Health sciences make improvements in nutrition all the time, but **low-fat, moderate-calorie intake is still the ideal and it always has been.** For example, antioxidants may be beneficial in guarding against cancer, but that doesn't change the fact that a healthy diet is still an important key to longevity. We've known all along that we get the vitamins we need if we eat the right foods. The current emphasis on new scientific discoveries causes us to get mired in details and forget the big picture.

However, **you certainly shouldn't ignore new ways of thinking about fitness,** dismissing them just because they seem new. For example, for years people thought that eating three square meals a day was the optimal diet. Now it's generally accepted that eating smaller, more frequent meals helps us to maintain our weight and gives us more energy. That's not a fad: it's common sense.

Subjective standards of health remain the same. **The ability to sustain sporting activity without getting winded was always a basic minimum standard of fitness**, and that isn't going to change anytime soon. But the fast-food mentality permeates the fitness world. Every advance is hot off the presses, every new product is "improved." "New" advances seem to arrive monthly, conveniently coinciding with magazine publication dates. It might come as a relief to know that you don't need to follow the latest craze.

Supplements

Diet supplements are increasingly available, but as Joe always says, "You like to eat, don't you?" Then **eat real foods not pills and capsules.**

Joe tells the story of a man starving in the desert. On his last gasp, he finally reaches a man who offers him a choice: a handful of vitamins, or a hot dog and a soda. Which one is he going to take? The vitamins won't save him. But even a hot dog and a soda, which have less nutrition than just about anything, will give him what he needs to survive. Eat whole, healthful foods and you won't need to supplement your diet.

Steroids

Without making any rash generalizations, I can tell you that most people you see in "fitness" magazines who display abnormally large muscles have probably resorted to illegal, harmful chemicals at some point to help them look that way.

Taking steroids is the worst kind of cheating. You're fooling yourself. It isn't you lifting the weight; it's you and the drugs. As soon as you stop taking the steroids, the gains you've made will disappear. If you **train drug-free you will keep your gains much longer.**

The point of fitness is to stay healthy. When you take steroids and other **dangerous supplements you put your health in danger.** And you find out only what you are capable of doing while you're taking the drugs. Discover what you can do by relying only on yourself.

Taper your meals.

I try not to eat before I go to the gym in the morning because I want my body to burn fat for energy when I exercise. Later, after my workout, I'll eat some foods high in carbohydrates. Then throughout the day, **I eat small meals, tapering off from carbs early in the day to protein later in the day to rebuild muscle. Don't eat late at night. Eat plenty of fruits and vegetables.** That's all you need to know.

Get a full night's sleep every night and you'll have plenty of energy the

next morning for your workout. Rely on your body—it's good enough.

One Goal:
Get Better
Every Day

People often wonder what I do to stay motivated, as if taking care of myself was unusual. For me, it's not a matter of having any special motivation. You don't think twice about brushing your teeth every day, you just do it. Taking care of things is second nature to most people. *Make taking care of your body part of your routine.*

This is the way I approach my training schedule. *The more you work out the easier it is to keep going. If you miss a day it's just that much harder to get back on track.* I view what I do as simply regular care and maintenance of my body.

Most people lead sedentary lives; modern conveniences don't require us to exert ourselves very often. Many of us could spend entire days sitting down without altering our lifestyles at all. So our bodies actually crave the exercise we give them. Our *heart, muscles, and lungs want to be challenged.*

Of course Joe helps me to stay extremely focused. I know he'll be there every morning, ready to give me that extra push. We've done this together for so long that we bring out the best in each other. That's why it's so helpful to work out with a trainer or training partner. You keep each other focused and your goals in sight.

Don't let your goals become your limits.

We all have the same goal: lifelong health and fitness. What you do today affects you for the rest of your life. *We're not training just for today, but for many years down the line.* We want to look and feel good right now, we want to look and feel good when we're seventy. Doing an extra set of crunches today is a building block that could still benefit you fifty years from now. Conversely, if you make the choice not to train today, that will affect you as well.

Our lives are the sum total of our daily actions. Whether these are positive, healthy actions or negative ones is for you to decide.

It's important to set goals, but don't let your goals become your limits. The problem with setting concrete goals in the gym comes when you achieve them. What do you do next?

It's human nature to ease off once we've accomplished our goals; thus our goals become our limits. Say you decide you'll run five miles by the end of the month. It seems a worthwhile goal but you're really just limiting yourself. Sure, you might run the five miles, but in the process you've created a mental barrier and kept yourself from seeing if you can really grow. *Why stop when you've accomplished your goal? Why not find out what you're really capable of?* You'll curtail your progress if you decide to pursue arbitrary goals. *Go as hard as you possibly can when you train, and the weights and distances will crumble in your path.*

Getting better every day

There is only one training goal that matters: striving for daily improvement. Vow to get better every day. Don't fall into the trap of dwelling on yesterday, or worrying about tomorrow; *worry about the present, what you can control right now.* Yesterday is gone, and tomorrow will be here soon enough. This applies to every facet of life, not just fitness. Use each day to improve your mind and your work, to improve your family and personal relationships. *Improve your life today and the future will take care of itself.*

At the old Muscle Beach in Santa Monica with my son, Jack.

Leave the little notebook at home.

I see people in the gym who record their entire workout in little notebooks. They carry them around and check off the exercises they've done. It's admirable that they take such a thorough approach to their workout. But the gym is not the place for pen and paper. If you're writing things down, you're not working out. Know what you're in the gym to do that day before you walk through the door.

Simply "going to the gym" is not a valid goal in itself. People go to the gym, they go to work, they go to school. *What's more important is to accomplish something while you're there.* Set yourself apart from the people who aspire only to "go" somewhere

You can't just go to the gym every day and hope that you'll improve once you get there. *You need a blueprint to build the foundation of fitness.* Joe and I approach our training sessions the way a contractor builds a house: we follow our blueprint, with the confidence that the blueprint will yield results. *We know exactly which muscles we'll be working each day. We work the upper body on days one, three, and five.* That could be Monday, Wednesday, and Friday or Tuesday, Thursday, and Saturday—it doesn't matter. *Choose the days that are most convenient for you.*

You use your legs a lot over the course of the week just to walk and get around. So we work our *legs two days a week*, on days two and four. *It's important to give each muscle group a full forty-eight hours of recovery.* We don't want to overtrain by taking a shortcut and working the same muscles on consecutive days.

We also know the order in which we'll work, from the largest muscles to the smallest. Chest and back for the upper body, or hamstrings and quads for the lower. You use your smaller muscles in every exercise you perform. You use your biceps and triceps when you work your chest. You use your forearms when you work your shoulders. *Smaller muscles require less work to maintain a tapered body. If you start with your smaller muscles they'll be worn out by the time you need your bigger muscles to lift bigger weights.*

Joe and I *come to the gym with a rough idea of how many exercises it will take to achieve muscle failure.* This number is different for every person. Ideally we like to complete eight to ten different exercises each for back and chest, and fewer for shoulders and arms. You can work your way up to this number and beyond.

This is the plan we have every time we walk into the gym. But after that, we just go. Once we start our workout we *don't stop to talk to anyone.* We *don't stop to wait in line* and we *don't stop to write in a notebook.* We're there with a specific purpose and we don't want to waste a minute of our time.

We *make use of every weight and machine that's available. If a machine isn't available, we move on to something that is.* This is why we *superset everything*, as I'll explain in the next chapter. We want to keep my heart beating the entire time to achieve maximum cardiovascular results.

There's no reason to set complicated training goals. You don't need to figure out how much weight to lift on every single exercise. *Intensity and correct form are*

much more important. Your body doesn't know how much weight you're lifting—it just knows when it's hard.

Focus on the moment; focus on the movement.

Plan your workout so you know exactly what needs to be done, ***but be flexible*** enough to work with whatever is available at your gym, then go for it. You'll have the confidence to keep going without stopping because you've done your planning and preparation beforehand.

Listen to your body. Let it tell you what you can do, and when it wants to do more, by all means, let it. If it tells you to ease off, you need to use less weight.

Take advantage of what works for you.

Everyone has something they use to give themselves that extra edge. Put the worst picture of yourself up on the refrigerator door to remind yourself to eat right. Or put on a pair of jeans that are too tight to remind yourself of the weight you'd like to be at. Post a saying or hang a picture on your wall that truly inspires you. Use any step to put you on the road to improvement. Don't neglect the simple motivational tools that are available to all of us: you know what works for you, so ***trust your instincts and use them.***

Take time for yourself. Then enjoy the rest of your day.

Everyone spends huge chunks of their day doing things for other people. Whether you're working for your boss, taking care of your kids, or hanging out with your friends, it's easy to neglect yourself. ***Try to make more time for yourself.*** And a good way to use that time is to improve your health and fitness for a few hours every week.

Ask yourself every day, did I get better today? Did I improve myself, my health, my fitness, some area of my life? If you did, congratulate yourself and enjoy the rest of your day. Then do it again tomorrow. That's the key to improvement.

True Mass Appeal:
A Lean, Trim Physique

We all want a lean, trim physique, with long, flexible muscles. Being slender makes us look better and feel better, but even more important, it contributes to our overall health and longevity. As we keep hearing, many Americans are overweight. Being overweight diminishes our self-confidence and leads to depression and lethargy. But ***we can get lean and stay lean once we commit to training for life.***

Cardiovascular exercise is one cornerstone of maintaining our ideal weight. We need to raise our heart rate, breathe deeply, and fill our lungs with oxygen for extended periods several times a week. For whatever reason, aerobic exercise and anaerobic exercise (weight training) are considered distinct and separate activities. I see people in the gym all the time who go through an entire workout without breaking a sweat. What's the point of work-

ing out if you don't make your heart and lungs stronger too? **Working out without breaking a sweat isn't working out at all.** Despite this obvious fact, most resistance training programs are anaerobic. That is, most people don't raise their heart rate high enough solely by lifting weights to gain any aerobic benefit from it.

We do. **Our workout combines weight training with an intense cardiovascular workout.** Focusing on these two simultaneously is the way to a lean, tapered body with long, flexible muscles.

Gyms usually divide the equipment into two different sections. Weights and machines over here, cardio equipment over there. It's as if the two should never meet. But by combining them you'll cut your workout time in half. **There's no reason to spend time stretching, then lift weights, and then go jogging for an hour later that afternoon. That's a waste of time, when you can get all the benefits of a full workout in an hour or less.**

Traditional weight training focuses on doing a few reps with heavy weights. As a result, the muscles need more time to recover and the chance of injury is greater. The entire pace of the workout slows down.

How much can you bench? Who cares?

Most people who begin weight training have their first experience with the bench press. Beloved by football coaches and teenage boys, **the bench press is the most overused move in bodybuilding.** It breeds the mentality of people standing around asking each other, "How much can you bench?" Men become obsessed with their bench-press totals, almost as if it were their income. All activity ceases around the bench as more and more plates are added—another excuse for people to stand around not working out.

Overuse of the bench press has effectively removed the "aerobic" from anaerobic exercise. People can't keep moving because they can't lift as much weight if they lift nonstop for an hour or more. They think they need to lift as much weight as possible to get a good workout. Get away from that mentality. **It's not how much weight you lift; it's how hard you work when you lift it.**

It's also difficult to get a cardio workout when you lift weights if you stick to a rigid workout plan. The machine you want to use next always seems to be tied up. Be flexible. Be ready to move on to something different. You'll see people sitting at the machines, resting between sets. You don't have to ask them to move, just go on to whatever is available, and **keep moving yourself.** Even the most crowded gym will have several machines available that no one uses. Make use of those machines and let the others stand in line.

Don't ruin all the hard work by overeating.

Of course, the most important way to control your weight is by watching what you eat. **Even the best exercise plan, closely followed, can be destroyed by eating too much of the wrong foods.** Eating a big dessert adds more calories than you could hope to burn **in an hour of intense exercise; an hour of your hard work can be destroyed in five minutes.** Which isn't to say you can't eat dessert. Just don't make it a daily habit. **Moderate caloric intake is still the best way to maintain your ideal weight.**

Burn calories in your sleep.

The key to maintaining a lean body is found in a deceptively simple equation: **Burn more calories than you take in and you'll lose weight.** But you shouldn't just count only the calories you burn while you exercise. You could never hope to burn the 2,000 to 3,000 calories you consume every day during the short time you're in the gym. So we need to be conscious of the ways our bodies use and burn calories.

You burn calories during exercise by training several times a week. **If you train intensely for an hour a day, five days a week, you can burn the equivalent of one pound worth of calories per week. You don't need to break out the calculator to realize that steady, regular exercise quickly adds up.** Who wouldn't like to burn four or five pounds every month? But you have to put in the time: five days a week, every week, for the rest of your life.

You also increase your resting metabolism by building muscle mass throughout your body. Every pound of muscle burns an extra 50 calories a week. Adding ten pounds of muscle will burn an extra 2,000 calories per month. **Add lean muscle and you'll burn calories in your sleep.**

The way Joe and I train takes advantage of all of these facts. And we do it without doing any extra cardiovascular activities. I don't run, bike, or swim unless it's for fun.

That extra edge: Work out in the morning.

The gym is never as crowded in the morning as it will be in the evening. That's because it's harder to work out in the morning. Working out in the morning is tough—and if it's tough to do, that's a good reason to do it.

If I start the day by taking care of myself, then I've got the rest of the day to go to work and do the things I have to do. When I was on *General Hospital* I had to be on the set at 7 o'clock in the morning. So I hit the gym at 4:30. People say they can't get up that early, that they're not a "morning person." Those are just more excuses. **Try going to bed a little earlier. Exercise in the morning so you're not wound up at night: you'll see how much easier it is to get up.**

Your heart, muscles, and lungs are freshest in the morning, since you've just had a full night's sleep. The daily stresses of work or school haven't taken their toll. Your mind isn't yet occupied. You're free to focus. The morning is the best time to put your body to the test.

Training early in the day has the added benefit of improving your metabolism throughout the rest of the day. **An intense workout can increase your body's natural ability to burn calories for up to twelve hours**. This points to another advantage of working out early in the day: as we start to consume our small meals, our body's ability to metabolize those calories will be greater if we've already been to the gym.

Save the big breakfast until after your workout.

*I try to **workout on an empty stomach for two reasons. Digestion consumes energy that your body could be putting into your workout. If you fill up before you train you won't achieve peak performance.*** So if you need something to get you going, keep it light.

You also force your body to burn fat for fuel by eating lightly or not at all before you train. Don't stock up on calories when you're trying to burn calories. Then if you continue to eat light meals throughout the day after getting your metabolism up by training hard and building muscle, your body will continue to burn fat instead of carbs.

A common misconception that is often used as an excuse is that an empty stomach will cause your body to burn muscle for energy. This is indeed a danger for endurance athletes, who have very low body fat. Those of us who train for shorter amounts of time have plenty of fat available for an hour's exertion. So unless you're a marathoner or a triathlete, don't use it as an excuse. ***Don't fill up before your workout, instead, force your body to burn through its fat reserves.***

There is a lot of focus in fitness journals on stretching. Stretching is certainly beneficial for someone who is sedentary or someone who is just starting a fitness program. But much of the reason for stretching separately is to compensate for improper movements inside and outside of the gym. ***Poor posture, sedentary lifestyles, and bad training habits are the real reasons that most people can't work out without stretching.***

Once you've started your workout you should be focusing on each individual movement, performing a full extension and contraction of each muscle. Don't lift more weight than you can handle without maintaining good form. And don't lift in short, jerky movements. ***Get a full extension and contraction on each lift, with moderate resistance, and feel those muscles stretch.***

The technique itself is simple: Don't stop.

From the time I do my first rep until I do my last, I ***don't rest for a second.*** I do each set fully and completely and when I've finished I immediately move on to the next set. This means that I'm lifting moderate weights for an hour or more. It's like aerobics, except that I have weights in my hands the entire time. ***Focus on sustaining maximum intensity throughout your workout. If you can't lift for a full hour then start with fewer exercises and gradually increase the number over time.***

The conventional workout aims for muscle failure for each muscle, and then moves on to exhaust the next muscle. But if we did that we wouldn't be able to continue long enough to burn many calories, or to obtain much cardiovascular benefit. We'd have to stop after a certain number of reps to rest the muscle. In the next chapter we'll see how it's possible to lift moderate to heavy weights for an hour or more without having to stop to rest. ***We do this by supersetting.***

Supersets:
Using Your Time Efficiently

You should be lifting weights continuously from the time you pick up that first weight until you finish. When you're done with a set, take a deep breath and half a second to think of the next exercise. Then move immediately to the next set. No stopping, no resting, no water breaks. Keep your heart pumping throughout the entire workout.

The only way to accomplish this is by allowing certain muscles to rest while we're working others. Supersetting incorporates the best of traditional bodybuilding concepts. That is, working muscles to failure, resting those muscles, then working them again. This allows us to keep our heart rate up, by working another muscle during the time we're resting the first muscle. And it lets us maintain a balance between the muscle groups by making sure one area isn't worked out of proportion to another. Using the exact same amount of opposing muscles of similar size ensures that they'll grow the same amount.

Symmetry is a common standard of beauty. When our arms, legs, and torso are in proportion, we simply look better, and that makes us feel better about ourselves. **Proportion** is also important to our health. We're most fit when our muscles are in **balance,** because every motion we make is a result of the cooperation of hundreds of different muscles. The simple motion of standing up requires a complex interaction of muscles from our shoulders to our legs.

Most people don't work out with this in mind. Certain areas of the body are neglected while others are overemphasized. They tend to concentrate on their chest at the expense of their back. **Overdeveloped forearms result in a "Popeye" look, and ruin the line from the shoulders to the wrists.** Many people ignore their legs completely. They may develop a well-defined torso, only to ruin the overall effect with a pair of spindly legs. This happens because people don't know how to train symmetrically and thoroughly.

We all have certain exercises that we like to do more than others. Some **men in particular may tend to work their chest and biceps almost exclusively. This is a vanity workout,** for looking good in a T-shirt, and doesn't do much to build overall health or fitness. It starts as a bad habit held over from adolescent weightlifting. If continued, the asymmetry will grow more pronounced from year to year. It may also cause health problems, particularly for the lower back. **For most men the lower back is the most important muscle they can work. Yet it is often the most neglected.**

Work muscles in logical groups.

You have to know your muscles in order to work them evenly. Think about symmetry: the back counterbalances the chest. The hamstring and quadriceps give definition to the front and rear of the upper leg, just like the triceps and biceps in the upper arm. Every muscle needs work, and every muscle, with few exceptions, has an opposite. If the opposite muscle gets the same amount of work you'll build muscle symmetrically. On the other hand, if you do six chest exercises for every back exercise, you'll build more muscle in front, which is bad for your posture and causes you to hunch over.

Some muscles pull and other muscles push. Almost every muscle has a counterpart that pulls or pushes in the opposite direction. For example, your chest pushes and your back pulls; thus your lower back and your abdominals work in tandem. **Being conscious of what muscles exert opposite movements is the key to supersetting.**

Supersetting makes your workout flow.

Once you understand the philosophy behind supersetting, the entire workout will fall into place. You'll realize that if you do leg presses (working your quadriceps), you'll need to follow it by doing something for your hamstrings. This could be a leg curl or some other exercise. Similarly, if you do a set of biceps curls, you'll need to counterbalance it by doing a set for your triceps. This could be a dip, a triceps extension, and so on. Whatever is available, grab it and go.

That's why **our workout is different every time. That's why we don't wait in line for a certain machine to become available. The muscle is what's important, not the specific machine or weight you use to work it.** There are probably a hundred different ways to work each muscle. Don't get bogged down deciding the

particular exercise you'll do: just do something.

We work opposite muscles in equal amounts to build our muscles in proportion. We also want to work them in a logical order. **All muscles are not created equal.** Some muscles are bigger than others are. Certain muscles are built for strength while others have more endurance. And don't forget that we use our smaller muscles to work our bigger muscles. We need to take all of these things into account when we devise our workout plan.

Supersets

Chest & Back

As I mentioned earlier, the pectoral muscles probably receive more attention than any other muscle, simply because we're more conscious of our chest than we are of our back, and because it's easier to train our chest—it's easier to push than to pull. There are plenty of excuses, but none of them will help your back get any stronger.

Our back keeps us upright. It gives us our posture, affecting the way we walk and the way we carry and present ourselves. It is absolutely essential for just about every movement we make. If you sit at a desk for most of the day your back may even be the only muscle you use to any significant degree. **Working your back should be a top priority** in the gym. It should get at least as much work as you do for your chest.

Shoulders

Our shoulders consist of three different muscles: the front, middle, and rear deltoids. We hit our front delts on most chest exercises and our middle delts by doing lateral arm raises. We work our rear delts during back exercises and by leaning forward to do arm raises. You can do a great superset for your delts with just a pair of dumbbells.

Arms

Our arms are not just biceps and triceps muscles, although those are certainly the biggest. We also want to work our forearms and the other muscle around the upper arm, the brachialis.

Legs

Our legs have biceps and triceps, the quadriceps and hamstrings. They perform the same functions as the muscles in our arms. Opening and closing, pushing and pulling. We do curls and extensions supersets with them just as we do for our arms.

Abdominals & Lower Back

Our abs and our lower back have more endurance than other muscles, and they recover faster. This is because they are constantly in use. So supersetting yours abs and lower back will require doing more reps in fewer sets. I only do one or two sets for my abs, but I do hundreds of reps. Of course I'm not going to train the lower back the way I do the rest of my back. Because I want my supersets to keep the balance between the two opposing muscle groups, I do hundreds of reps for my lower back just as I do for my abs.

Think Before You Train

It's not which exercises we do that make us successful; it's how we do them. Using **proper technique allows the exercise to do its job by working the correct muscles**. Don't just go through the motions when you train. When we're in the gym we shouldn't be thinking about other things. Your mind won't help you if you let it drift elsewhere. **Focus all of your attention on the task at hand.**

Remove the distractions.

When Joe and I are in the gym we don't want any distractions. That's why you'll see me wearing dark glasses in the gym. After the workout, Joe and I are as friendly as can be, and I'm happy to chat with people, sign autographs—whatever. But during the workout, people need to understand that we're there for one reason. We're there to get better. And if we lose that chance, by getting distracted or stopping to chat, we'll never get it again. That day is gone; it's a write-off. **Every day is valuable.** I don't write days off.

       We don't listen to music. Consciously or subconsciously, music affects the way you train. Music lessens your concentration. We want to be able to focus a hundred percent on what we're doing. If we're tapping our foot to a song, we're not concentrating. **People who are used to listening to music in the gym eventually come to rely on it for their power. Rely on yourself.**

Don't make things easier. Make them harder.

Difficulty makes us better. We need to struggle to improve, avoiding the path

of least resistance. So we don't look for ways to make things easier, we look for ways to make them harder.

I don't wear gloves or a support belt when I lift. They're crutches. People wear belts because they're attempting to lift more weight than their lower back can support. Joe and I concentrate on strengthening the lower back and using less weight. The same goes for gloves: lift what you can lift barehanded and let your body adapt.

Create a schedule that works for you.

I train my upper body on Mondays, Wednesdays, and Fridays, and I train my lower body on Tuesdays and Thursdays. Then I take the weekend off, to let my body recuperate, to play with my son, and have fun. But this isn't set in stone. Switch your workout around to suit your schedule. You could even train less, doing upper body on Mondays and Fridays and lower body on Wednesdays. You'll still benefit from the effort if you go at it hard enough.

It doesn't matter how much work you do. It's how much work you do correctly and with maximum intensity. *If your attention is starting to wander, if you're thinking about other things, you may still be doing the exercise, but you won't be doing the best that you can do. When that happens, start over and concentrate throughout the set.*

Train quickly, but lift slowly.

Just because we superset doesn't mean we race through each exercise to get to the next. The opposite is true. The exercises themselves are what make us sweat, not the lack of rest breaks between sets. Getting to the next machine is only a matter of a few steps. Controlling the resistance once we get there is what makes our heart pump.

That means performing each exercise as methodically as possible. *Maintain correct form throughout the lift, not just for half of it.* Remember that the negative portion of the lift, lowering the weight, is just as important as raising it. Control the weight in both directions, don't let the weight control you—and don't let gravity give you a boost when you should be doing it yourself.

When you think you can't do anymore, that's when the workout starts.

We talked about the dangers of setting concrete goals. Never is that more apparent than when you're reading a list of exercises in a book or a magazine. You might think to yourself, I can do that. What you should be thinking is I can do more than that. So *don't get in a rut with three sets, four sets, or any predetermined number. Do as much as you can do, and when you think you can't do anymore, that's when the workout starts.*

However, it's important that you *don't overtrain*. Don't wear your body down so much in one session that you're laid out for a week. *Consistency is still the key.* Just don't put limits on what you can do. Forget about the structure of working out, the weights, the sets and all of that. When you forget how many sets you've done because you're concentrating so hard on getting the most out of them, that's progress. *Focus on yourself and what you're doing right now.*

WORKOUT

Days One, Three, and Five:

UPPER BODY

The workouts that follow are examples of the types of exercises I do every day. But if you follow this list step by step, you are missing the point. I'm not going to make it that easy. After you've read the basic principles, ***use your knowledge of your own situation and your own body to create the workout for yourself.***

The muscles we work don't change, but the exercises do change—daily, weekly, and monthly. ***The more different kinds of exercises you do, the more you'll improve.*** We want to prevent our body from falling into a routine, to force it to grow. If we do the same exercises every time, our workouts get boring. ***Each trip to the gym should be an adventure into the unknown. Do something you've never done before. Mix up the workout each time. Challenge yourself.***

For example, Joe and I normally work the biggest muscles first and finish with the smaller ones, starting with the chest and finishing with our forearms. But having made that rule, sometimes we break it. Once in a while we'll start with the smaller muscles and move up to the biggest. Or we'll do each exercise as one long continuous set with dozens of reps. Sure it's hard. And it's not the right way to train every day. But it breaks us out of the routine and makes the workout a challenge.

These are just guidelines. It's up to you to follow the guidelines and make them your own. Be creative. You may not have the same machines in your gym. You may not even go to a gym. It doesn't matter. You could get the same workout from doing pushups, pullups,

squats, and lunges. Going to the gym is just one way to train, a means to an end. What's important is to work every muscle.

Some people use free weights exclusively and some always use machines. We use both, since either way we will get results. However, there are some advantages to using machines. Because we are also doing an intense cardio workout by doing supersets, machines allow us to do more exercises with less chance of injury.

Remember that muscles are composed of thousands of fibers, bundled together. So when we say we're working the muscle, we are actually trying to work each individual fiber in the muscle. The angle and range of motion of the exercise determines which fibers we use. The more diverse the exercises for each muscle, the more those fibers will grow.

We haven't included the amount of any resistance with these exercises. Everybody is different, and you'll soon know what you can lift. Follow this guideline, though: *start with far less weight than you think you will need. Most people have no idea how tough it is to superset until they get out there and do it.*

Chest & Back

The various muscles of *the chest and back are perfect examples of opposing muscle groups, as they perform movements that counteract each other.* The chest pushes and the back pulls. It isn't complicated.

The chest consists of two large muscles, pectoralis major and minor. These muscles are attached by tendons to the upper forearm, and contract to pull the arms forward and across the torso. Whether we do presses, flys, or pushups, all chest exercises are a variation on this pushing motion.

Different parts of the muscle are required to pull the arm at different elevations across the body. Raise your arm over your head and feel how the upper pectorals engage to pull the arm forward. Now lower your hand to waist high and perform the same movement. This time the bottom of the chest performs the contraction. A good chest exercise program finds ways to engage all parts of the chest muscles by varying the angle of the repetition.

The upper back muscles perform similar but opposite functions in terms of pulling the arms away from the body. The back consists of three main muscles that work together. The latissimus dorsi, which run down each side of the back, are large muscles responsible for most pulling movements. Below the neck, the trapezius muscles shrug the shoulders. And below them in the middle of the back, the rhomboids pull the shoulder blades together. The two main types of back exercises, rows and pulldowns, work all of the muscles in the group.

We've selected six exercises each for back and chest, to be performed in supersets. That *doesn't mean that you should limit yourself to these.* There might be thirty different exercises for back and chest that you can do in the gym, and all of them are valuable. You should try to get to all of them at some point over the course of your training. These machines just happen to be situated close together in my own gym, so I choose these exercises because I can keep my intensity high and my heart pumping.

See what's available in your gym and plan accordingly. Mix and match the supersets by pairing up different exercises, then vary your workout by switching the combinations.

Upright Machine Row

Any of the upright row machines like the t-bar will work the back, as well as the shoulders and biceps. Squeeze your shoulder blades together for a peak contraction. Then slowly extend the arms forward until you feel a deep stretch in your back.

Pec Deck

Go immediately to the pec deck. This exercise increases the size of your pectorals. Press forward until the pads or handles meet and hold for a second, feeling it in the very center of the chest. Then control the weight as you return to the original position, shoulder blades together.

Lat Pulldown (Regular Grip)

Pulldowns are a great way to increase width and build the V shape in your back. The different combinations of pulldowns are endless and I incorporate several into each workout. Experiment with different handles and grips to vary your training. A wide grip works the upper lats more; a narrow grip works the lower lats. Turn your palms up or use another bar with palms facing each other (refer to the photo). Bring the bar down in front of you, not behind you. Since we perform these exercises quickly, we want to do anything we can to prevent injury. When you finish a set here, go immediately to the incline bench press machine.

Lat Pulldown (Alternate Grip)

>>

>>

Incline Bench Machine Press

Use the incline bench press machine to target your upper chest. Concentrate on controlling the weight in the positive *and* negative directions; don't let gravity do the work for you.

10

Upright Cable Row

Whether you use dumbbells, barbells, or cables, upright rows are great for working the trapezius muscles, as well as the shoulders. Pause a second at the top of each rep for a peak contraction. Flys isolate the chest muscles and require less dependence on the triceps than many chest exercises. By sitting at an incline, we work the fibers that need it most, at the top of the chest muscles. Move the dumbbells in a semicircular motion to get the optimum range of movement.

>>

Incline Dumbbell Fly

>>

V
V

Assisted Pullup

Pullups give incredible definition to the back, while also working the shoulders, brachialis, and biceps. Do these reps slowly and carefully to avoid shoulder injury. Again, you should experiment with different grips each time you do pullups, in order to target different areas of your back. >>>

<<

Flat Bench Machine Press

Here we combine pullups with the flat bench press. Despite its reputation there is still no better way to build the size of the chest. Using a machine press allows me to maintain the fast pace of the workout without resting or waiting for a spotter. Remember to control the weight in both directions.

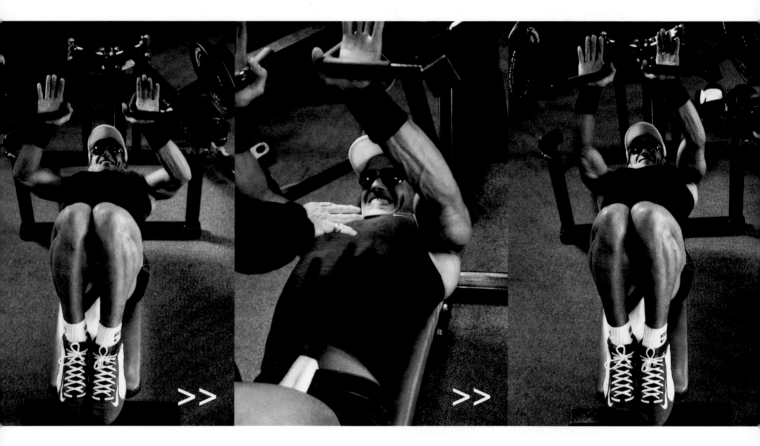

Seated Row

To maximize the effects of the seated row, keep your knees bent and concentrate on feeling this exercise throughout the full range of motion. Extend forward from the hips at the start, and we also work the important lower back. You could do seated rows using only your shoulders and biceps if you use incorrect form, so be careful to avoid this mistake.

Superset rows with cable crossovers. This exercise really brings out the striations in the upper pectorals for a well-defined chest. It also works the shoulders. Bend your knees, lean slightly forward, and cross your arms until your hands overlap.

Cable Crossover

>>

>>

Pushup

You can also do pulldowns using the same equipment from the last set. Kneel on the ground to isolate your back and shoulders. Pull the cables in until your hands are shoulder high, then hold it for a second until you really feel it burn.

Then it's time to hit the ground for some pushups. Old-fashioned pushups are still a great way to work your upper body, and you don't need any equipment at all. If I'm on location for a

Cable Pulldown

>>

movie and don't have access to a gym, doing pushups in my trailer keeps me ready to face Joe the next time I'm in the gym. Again, keep switching from narrow to wide grips to target different muscle fibers. This list could go on, and when I work out it does. But you get the point: **the chest and back contain the biggest muscles in the upper body, so they get the most work.** We've also used our shoulders quite a bit, but we still need to train them individually.

Shoulders

The shoulder is particularly suited to supersets because, like with the chest and back, it's important to prevent imbalances before they happen. And just like the back, the rear shoulder is often neglected as well.

How can you superset the shoulder, you might ask, since it's only a single muscle? The shoulder has three "heads," the front, middle, and rear deltoids. The front deltoid gets a tremendous amount of work during the chest exercises. So we train the shoulders so that the rear and middle deltoids get an equal amount of work by doing a shoulder tri-set that works all three heads. This shoulder workout, combined with the fat burning of the supersets, will build incredible definition in your shoulders without adding too much bulk.

Do all shoulder exercises slowly and carefully to avoid rotator cuff injuries.

Shoulder Press

The shoulder press targets the middle, or medial, deltoids. Slowly lift the weight overhead until you reach full extension, then hold it a moment before controlling it all the way down. Don't allow the weight to come to rest at the bottom of the rep. Raise it back up immediately.

Have a pair of dumbbells waiting for you when you've finished the presses. You're ready to do some back flys.

Back Fly

Your shoulders should be burning from the last set so you'll probably use very light weight. The back fly is a great exercise for isolating those difficult rear deltoids. Sit down and bend forward at the hips and tuck your chin in, then raise your shoulders with your arms slightly bent. Hold it, then slowly lower the weight back down.

Finally, stand up holding the same dumbbells and do some lateral raises, returning your attention to the middle delts. Slowly raise your arms in a semicircle, and hold them at the top for a second to isolate the muscle. Then lower your arms, controlling the weight all the way down.

>>

VV

Lateral Dumbbell Raise

>>

>>

Arms

We've worked from chest to back to shoulders so far, but we've used our arms the entire time. So our arm workout will incorporate fewer exercises than we used for our shoulders, and far fewer than for the bigger muscles. However, **there is still plenty of work to do because the arms have several smaller muscles that need training.**

There are five muscles in the arms worth discussing here. The biceps and triceps are opposites, closing and opening the arm. Likewise, the forearm flexor and extensor muscles move the wrist in opposite directions. And we don't neglect the muscle that runs along the middle of the upper arm, the brachialis. Five muscles mean five different exercises. We can combine them into one giant set with the E-Z curl bar.

>> >>

Slowly, with your palms
facing up, curl your
wrists up and down
while holding the bar in
a narrow grip to work
the forearm flexors.

V
V

Turn your hands over in a wide grip and bend your wrist in the opposite direction to work the forearm extensors.

101

Triceps Extension (Curl Bar)

Triceps Extension (Dumbbell)

The closer together you keep your hands, the more you'll isolate the triceps. We modify this exercise by using dumbbells.

Biceps Curl
3–4 SETS OF EACH, 8–12 REPS PER SET

>>

Biceps Curl (Curl Bar)

>>

Stand with your hands held shoulder width apart on the bar. Remember that lowering the weight is just as important to your biceps as raising it. Again, we can also do biceps curls with dumbbells and sometimes do both to mix it up.

When we finish with the arms we're done with the upper body. As you can see, we do a lot of work. ***But by doing supersets you should be able to finish all of these exercises in about 45 minutes.*** We still have abs left to do, but first let's look at the lower body workout.

Biceps Curl (Dumbbell)

Brachialis (not pictured)
3–4 SETS OF EACH, 8–12 REPS PER SET

This exercise is like a standing biceps curl but with the palms
facing downward and the arms spread wide. Curl the arms
upward to work the brachialis.

WORKOUT
Days Two and Four:
LOWER BODY

We tend to work our lower body much more in everyday life than our upper body. Whether it's walking, hiking, or climbing stairs, we always have plenty of opportunities to use our legs. So we train our legs two days a week instead of three. *We also train them somewhat differently than we train the upper body, in that we do more supersets with the same muscles, rather than with the opposites.*

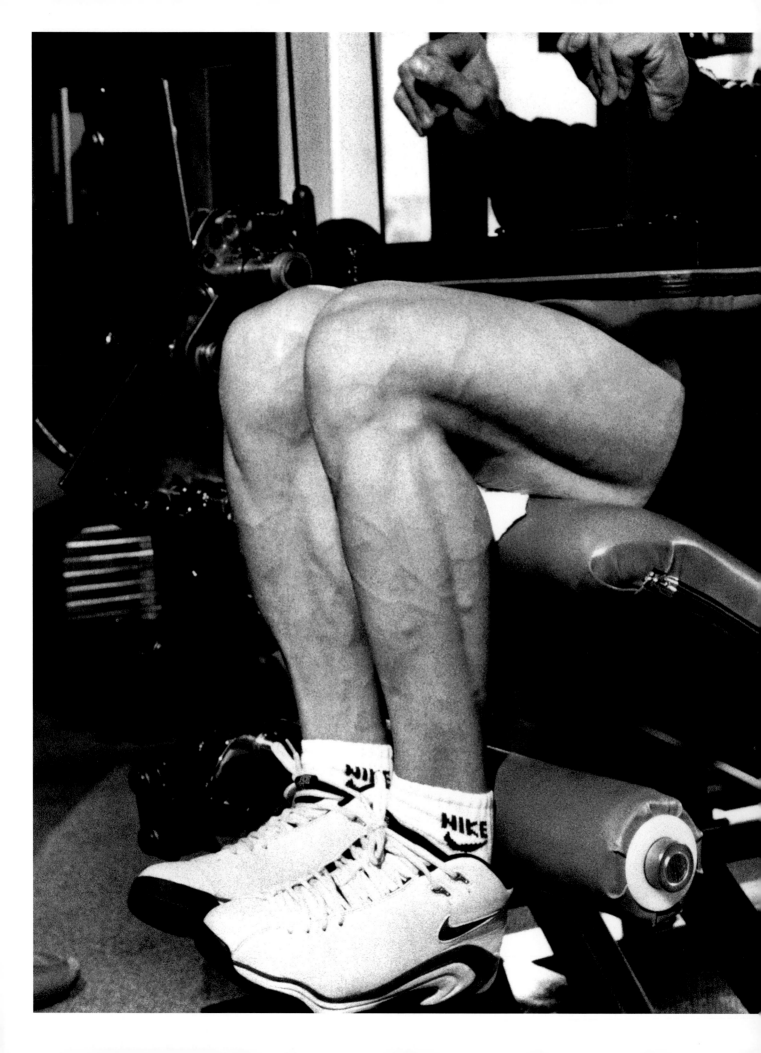

Legs

Legs are designed for incredible endurance. They are also designed to support heavy weight. They support our own body weight all day, every day. You couldn't do pushups of your body weight for more than a few minutes without tiring. Put that same weight atop your legs however, and you could walk twenty miles if you had to. So **we have to find more intense training methods to make the legs grow.**

Muscle growth in our legs is important because our glutes, quads, and hamstrings are large muscles by nature. Add too much muscle in your neck and your overall appearance will be out of proportion. But add muscle in the legs and it is far less noticeable. So **the lower body is definitely an area where we should look to add a few pounds of muscle to increase our metabolism—and our strength.**

The range of motion that governs the major leg muscles is so limited that the workout is fairly simple. What we can do with our legs is similar to what we can do with our arms. Our legs can just do a whole lot more of it. But just because the workout is simple doesn't mean it's easy. Our legs are capable of handling a lot of work, so they require a workout of greater intensity.

There are three major muscles in the legs: quadriceps, hamstrings, and calves. Joe and I do tri-sets for the legs, with one exercise for each muscle. Choose one exercise below for each muscle and do three or four sets of each, alternating one set per muscle. Then choose three more exercises and do them. For example, you could do leg extensions, leg curls, and seated calf raises. Then you could do leg presses, seated leg curls, and standing calf raises. Working the muscles in that order allows your quads to rest while you're working your hamstrings and calves, and vice versa. It also keeps the legs balanced and symmetrical.

Quadriceps

The quadriceps are composed of four different muscles that run parallel to each other. So **we need to vary our exercises to keep all four balanced and toned.** The direction your toes are pointed has a lot to do with determining which muscle fibers will perform the reps. I do three or four supersets for the quads that combine every possible variation on the leg press, the squat, and the leg extension.

Leg Press (Flat)

The leg press isolates the thighs even better than the squat. Here I'm using both the flat and 45-degree leg presses. The angle of the press isn't as important as the placement of the feet and the direction the toes are pointed. Place the feet lower on the plate to work the quads, higher to work the glutes. And if we point the toes inward on a set, it will work the inner quads more. >>

Leg Press (Toes Pointed Inward)

Leg Press (45 Degree)

Squat

>> This squat machine is another variation on the traditional squat. Using the machine allows us the benefits of the squat rack, with the ease of use required for supersets.

Leg Extensions

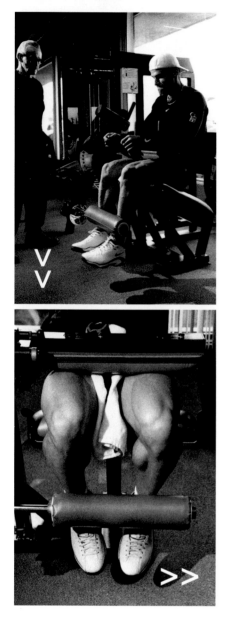

I like to alternate between one- and two-legged leg extensions. Using one leg at a time prevents the weaker leg from letting the stronger leg carry the load. Work the leg extension slowly, concentrating on the positive and negative movements equally, controlling the weight in both directions. Hold at the top for a peak contraction.

Supersetting with these different machines will produce an intense thigh burn. Enjoy it. It means your legs are getting stronger.

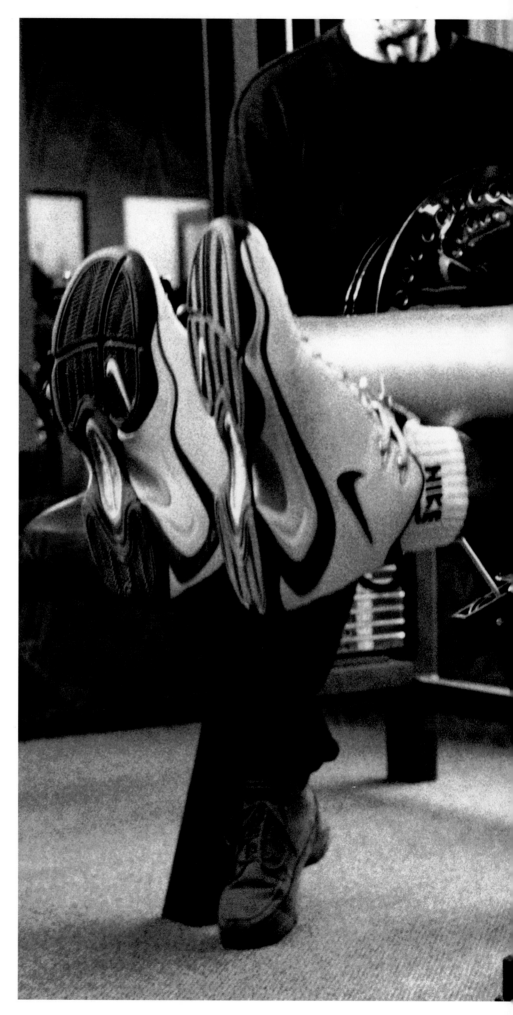

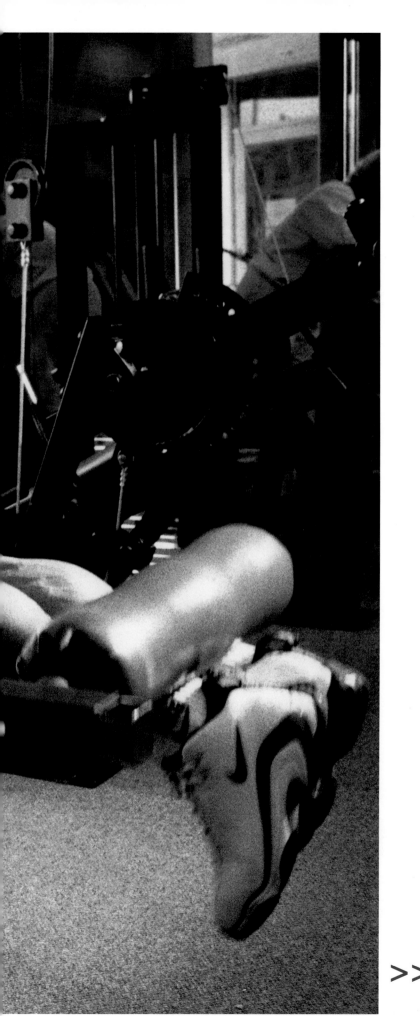

Hamstring & Gluteus

The back of the thigh, or hamstring, which consists of three different muscles, bends the leg back from a straight position. For many people this can be a problem area for tightness and cramps, so be sure to stretch your hamstrings out by fully extending on each rep.

The gluteus muscles engage the lower back to propel our legs forward. We use them in almost every hamstring exercise, then we use the glute isolator to focus on them even more.

>>

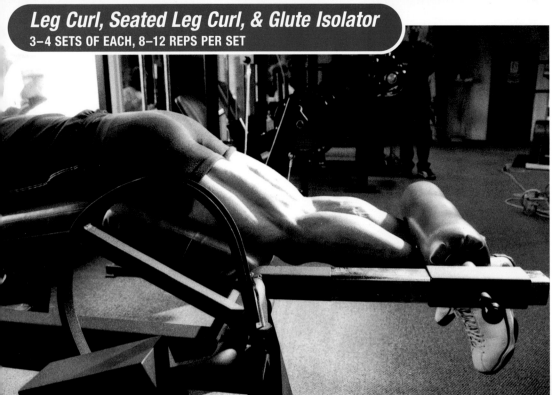

Leg Curl

The regular leg curl lets me work the lower part of the hamstring, while the seated machine works the muscle near the top.

Seated Leg Curl

Glute Isolator

Although we work the glutes during the hamstring exercises, the glute isolator allows us to feel the burn all the way up to the top of the rear thigh.

Calves

With the exception of your heart, your calves probably have more endurance than any other muscle in your body. Every step you take is initiated by a calf contraction. That's thousands of reps every day and they still don't get tired unless you walk or run several miles. So your calves need some intense training in order to improve.

Standing Calf Raise

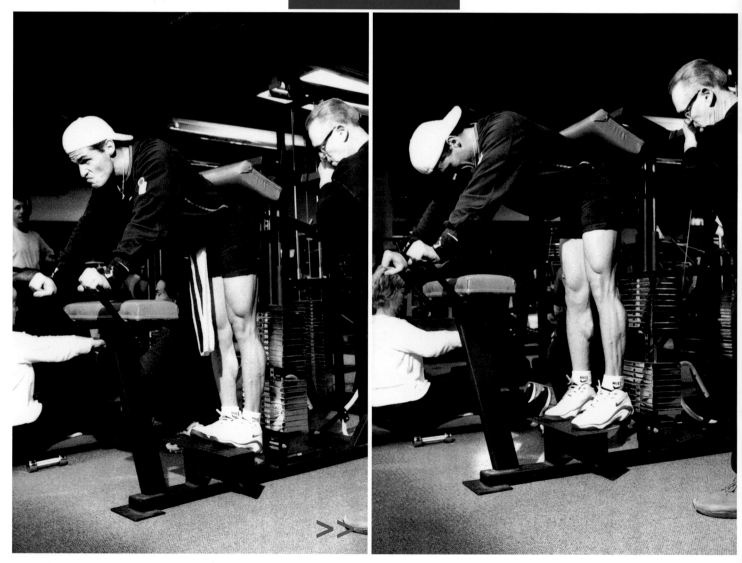

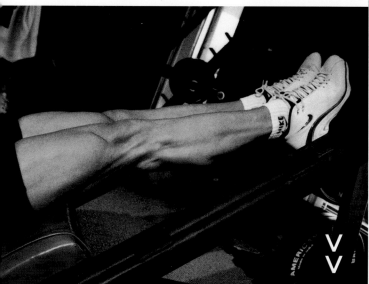

Seated Calf Raise

Do calf raises slowly to get the most intensity from your reps. Lower your body slowly as far as it will go, feeling the entire length of the stretch. Then lift it as high as you can go. Work every fiber in the calf, from top to bottom. I alternate standing and seated raises, and vary the position of my toes from set to set, working the muscle from side to side.

125

At this point, if you've trained correctly, your legs should be wobbling like jelly. And that's when you need to remind yourself that the workout is just beginning. I like to finish my leg days by doing some standing leaps. After you've worked every muscle in your leg individually, work them all together to go that extra step. Crouch down low until your knees are fully bent, then uncoil like a spring, jumping as high as you possibly can. We also do this exercise holding 10- or 15-pound weights.

I haven't touched on the groin muscles, and I haven't mentioned the shins. If you think that means I don't train these muscles then you haven't been paying attention. **The human body has more than five hundred muscles. Train everything.** Following the basic program I've outlined simply gives you the best shot at covering them all.

The body is like a chain, only as strong as its weakest link. Your weakest muscle determines the strength of your entire body, so don't leave a single muscle fiber untouched.

Congratulations if you've done the best that you can possibly do to strengthen your legs today. Now it's time to move to the last two areas of the body, the lower back and the abdominals.

WORKOUT
ABDOMINALS
AND LOWER BACK

Every muscle is important, but none are more crucial than our lower back and abs. We use them in virtually every single thing we do. They support the spine and give us our posture. This in turn governs the way we look, the way we carry ourselves, and the way we feel.

These muscles are very important to maintaining a healthy physique. It isn't much of a stretch to draw a straight line from abdominal and lower back training to improved self-confidence and happiness. Nagging lower back pain prevents us from any number of activities. *A tight stomach and a healthy lower back give us a feeling of confidence that is tough to match.* Don't neglect these muscles at the end of your training day. If you tend to go overtime, cut something else out if you have to, but don't ignore these two.

Abdominals

No amount of abdominal exercises can compensate for a poor diet. *The most ripped washboard won't show if there is a layer of fat over it. The best way to flatten your stomach will always be by burning calories and eating the right foods.* Still, some people will never have a washboard stomach, as fat storage in the stomach is more pronounced in certain people. But appearance isn't the issue here: train your abs for health and fitness, to improve your posture and your self-confidence.

Abdominals recover quickly, so they are the only body part I work every day of the week. I do at least 1,000 reps of both of the following exercises, sometimes many more. Do as many as you can.

>>

Seated Balanced Leg Raise Crunch (Bench Crunch)

Seated Balanced Leg Raise Crunch

(Crunches with Obliques)

The main problem with sit-ups and ab machines is that without total concentration and proper form you'll work everything but the abs. The only way to avoid using your quads, lower back, and hip flexors is to stay focused. Concentrate on feeling the crunch all the way from top to bottom.

Any of the various crunch exercises or leg raises are good at isolating the abs. I do seated crunches / leg raises on the bench for two reasons. First, regular crunches are great for the upper abdominal muscles, but I don't feel the lower abs working as much. The reverse is true for leg raises. But when I sit up on the bench and combine the two, crunching from the top and lifting from the bottom, I feel the burn throughout the abdominals. Second, not using my hands for balance makes the exercise harder, and puts extra stress on the whole midsection. I sometimes like to vary the movement by twisting my obliques in midcrunch.

Obliques

We want to maximize the ratio of our shoulders to our waist, so we want the waist to get smaller, not larger. Overtraining the obliques adds thickness to the waist. Focus on toning and shortening the obliques with quick, sharp movements.

Side Bends

1–2 SETS, 1000–2000 REPS

Do short, quick side bends, standing with your hands on your hips. Keep your legs stationary so you only bend at the hips. And don't use any extra weight to do your oblique exercises—we don't want to build more muscle; we just want to tone what's already there.

Lower Back

The lower back is another area that we don't train for appearance. No one has ever won a fitness contest solely on the basis of his or her lower back. On the other hand, millions of people complain of lower back pain every year. And of course, this can be prevented through proper training.

Strengthen the lower back when you're young, in early adulthood. The longer you wait, the more chance that injuries will interfere with your training, and there is no injury more harmful to training than chronic lower back pain.

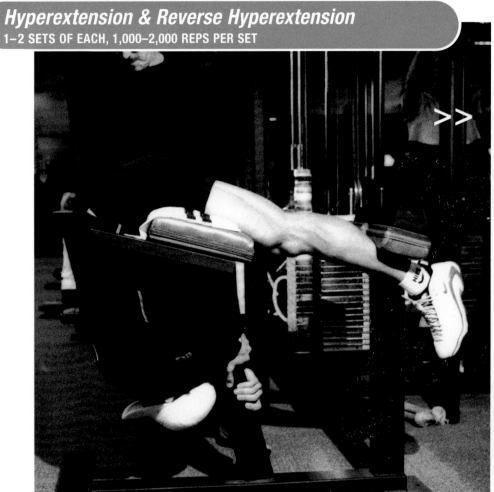

>>

Hyperextension

<<

Joe and I do lower back exercises on the same days as legs. Together with abdominal exercises they provide support and improved posture. We do hyperextensions on the special benches pictured, both by extending the trunk and extending the legs. **Build strength slowly and consistently in your lower back to prevent injury.**

I did not include guidelines for sets and reps for the abs and lower back. You should do at least one set of each, doing enough reps that you exhaust the muscles. This amount will be different for everyone. Do them until you think you can't do anymore, then keep going.

Reverse Hyperextension

12

Sooner or Later, Only Health Matters

I've been following this program for three years now, and it has exceeded my expectations in every way. I've stayed lean but gotten stronger. I've added muscle without sacrificing flexibility. I've been ready for every sports activity and opportunity I've been presented with. And my aerobic conditioning is so good that when I have the physical exam that's required before starting work on each movie, the doctors always ask me if I do a lot of cardiovascular exercise. No extra cardio, I say, just five intense workouts a week.

I enjoy a massage every week to relieve stress and help my muscles recuperate. While I haven't been injured, I also have regular appointments with my physical therapist, Carlos Rodriguez. He has also noticed significant changes in my body over the last three years.

The workout I've described in this book gives you room to grow. It can be the beginning of a serious approach to fitness for anyone; it can also be a lifelong exercise program for the most demanding athlete.

Even if you start with only a few of the ideas I've outlined in this book, you'll be building a foundation of fitness, to which you can keep adding elements one by one, noticing the change the program makes in your life.

Stop making excuses for your health, for the way you look, and for the

way you feel. Take pride in this wonderful gift that we have been given. Take control of your own destiny by doing something now. Don't wait until tomorrow to do something about it.

Start today.

No more excuses.